FROM SEA to SHINING SEA

VIRGINIA

GINA DE ANGELIS

Consultants

MELISSA N. MATUSEVICH, PH.D.
Curriculum and Instruction Specialist
Blacksburg, Virginia

MARGE ROZUM
Librarian, Woolridge Elementary School
Midlothian, Virginia

CHILDREN'S PRESS®
A DIVISION OF SCHOLASTIC INC.

New York • Toronto • London • Auckland • Sydney • Mexico City
New Delhi • Hong Kong • Danbury, Connecticut

Virginia is located in the southeastern part of the United States. It is bordered by North Carolina, Tennessee, Kentucky, West Virginia, Maryland, Washington, D.C., and the Atlantic Ocean.

Project Editor: Meredith DeSousa
Art Director: Marie O'Neill
Photo Researcher: Marybeth Kavanagh
Design: Robin West, Ox and Company, Inc.
Page 6 map and recipe art: Susan Hunt Yule
All other maps: XNR Productions, Inc.

Library of Congress Cataloging-in-Publication Data

De Angelis, Gina.
    Virginia/ by Gina De Angelis.
      p. cm.—(From sea to shining sea)
    Includes bibliographical references and index.
    ISBN 0-516-22313-5
    1. Virginia—Juvenile literature. [1. Virginia.] I. Title. II. From sea to shining sea (Series)

F226.3 .D43 2001
975.5—dc21   00-065960

TABLE of CONTENTS

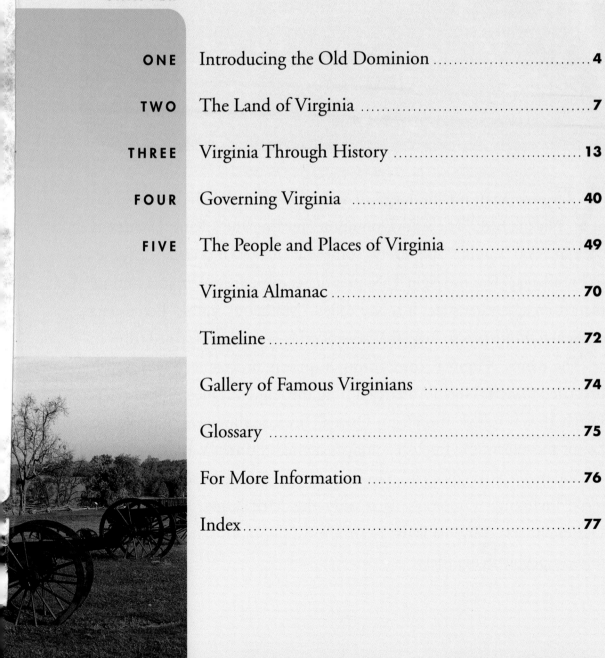

CHAPTER ONE

INTRODUCING THE OLD DOMINION

During Christmastime, the boardwalk in Virginia Beach is lit from end to end with 500,000 lights.

Virginia may not be large in size, but it's definitely big in spirit. Nicknamed "The Old Dominion" by England's King Charles II back in 1660, Virginia also has two other nicknames. It is called "Mother of Presidents," because eight U.S. presidents came from Virginia—more than from any other state. It is also called "Mother of States," because its original territory was so huge that several other states were formed from it.

The name "Virginia" comes from a queen's nickname. The English first tried to settle North America during the reign of Queen Elizabeth I. Elizabeth was called "the Virgin Queen" because she never married. To honor the queen, the English colonists named the area Virginia.

Today, Virginia covers 42,326 square miles (109,624 square kilometers), including waterways. It is only the 35th largest state in area. Despite its size, Virginia is the twelfth most populous state, with over 7 million people living there.

Virginia is most famous for its long history. It is the oldest English settlement in North America. Every year, thousands of people visit Virginia's historic sites, such as Jamestown and Colonial Williamsburg, Revolutionary War sites, and Civil War battlefields.

What comes to mind when you think of Virginia?

* Four of America's first five presidents, including Virginians George Washington and Thomas Jefferson
* Colonial life in historic Williamsburg
* Sand and surf at Virginia Beach
* Race car drivers speeding around Richmond International Raceway
* Hiking and biking in the Blue Ridge Mountains
* Caves with ancient rock formations
* Historic battlegrounds and national monuments
* Chincoteague ponies running free on Assateague Island
* Ships, aircrafts, and submarines being built at Newport News Shipbuilding

What kind of place is Virginia? What is the land like? Who lives there? Read on, and find out!

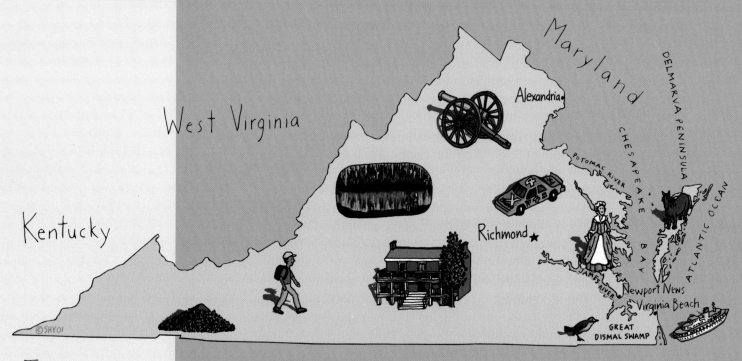

Maryland

DELMARVA PENINSULA

West Virginia

Alexandria

CHESAPEAKE

POTOMAC RIVER

BAY

ATLANTIC OCEAN

Kentucky

Richmond ★

JAMES RIVER

Newport News

Virginia Beach

©SHY01

GREAT
DISMAL SWAMP

Tennessee

North Carolina

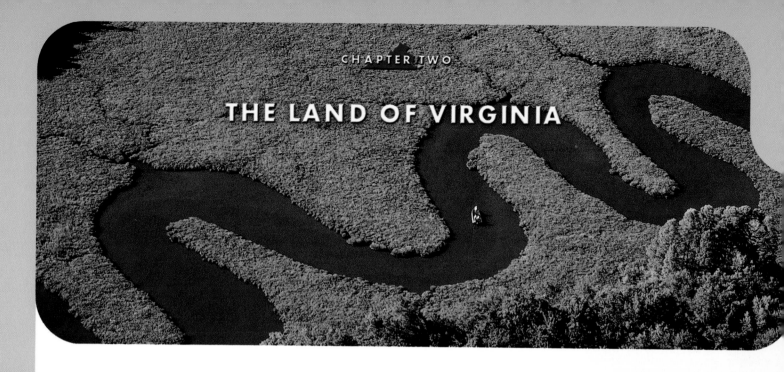

CHAPTER TWO

THE LAND OF VIRGINIA

Virginia is located on the east coast of North America. Virginia shares borders with North Carolina in the south, Tennessee and Kentucky in the southwest, West Virginia in the northwest, and Maryland and Washington, D.C. in the northeast. The Atlantic Ocean borders Virginia on the east.

Virginia can be divided into five geographic regions. They are the Tidewater, Piedmont, Blue Ridge Mountains, Ridge and Valley, and Appalachian Plateau. In the eastern part of Virginia is the Tidewater region, a coastal plain with wide, slow-moving rivers flowing into the Chesapeake Bay. To the west, the Piedmont includes the land between the Tidewater and the Blue Ridge Mountains, the third region. The Ridge and Valley is west of the Blue Ridge Mountains, and the Appalachian Plateau covers the southwestern corner of the state.

The James River flows through all of Virginia's geographic regions except the Appalachian Plateau.

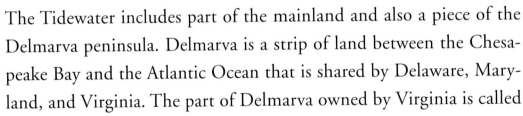

The Tidewater includes part of the mainland and also a piece of the Delmarva peninsula. Delmarva is a strip of land between the Chesapeake Bay and the Atlantic Ocean that is shared by Delaware, Maryland, and Virginia. The part of Delmarva owned by Virginia is called the Eastern Shore. It is connected to the Virginia mainland by the Chesapeake Bay Bridge-Tunnel—a series of bridges and tunnels that is more than seventeen miles long! Some of Virginia's largest cities are located in the Tidewater region on the mainland, including Virginia Beach, Norfolk, Newport News, and Hampton.

Just south of these cities lies the Great Dismal Swamp, a large wetland. Over 200 species of birds, about 80 species of snakes, frogs and turtles, and mammals such as otters, bats, raccoons, mink, foxes, and squirrels all live in the Dismal Swamp.

Dismal Swamp is a haven for birds and mammals. Many rare plants can be found there, as well.

THE PIEDMONT

The Piedmont, west of the Tidewater region, is the largest geographic region in Virginia. Separating Tidewater from the Piedmont is a Fall Line. The land is about 850 feet (259 meters) higher to the west of the Fall Line, causing waterfalls and river rapids.

Many rivers flow through the Piedmont, from the west or northwest to the east. These rivers include the Potomac, Rappahannock, and Pamunkey in the north. The James and Appomattox Rivers flow through central Virginia. The Nottoway, Meherrin, Roanoke, and Dan Rivers are in the south.

Several cities, like Richmond, Petersburg, Alexandria, and Fredericksburg developed along the Fall Line. The northern Piedmont, around Washington, D.C., is Virginia's most crowded area. Some of the cities in northern Virginia are Arlington, Falls Church, Manassas, and Fairfax.

Richmond, the state's capital, sits along the James River.

9

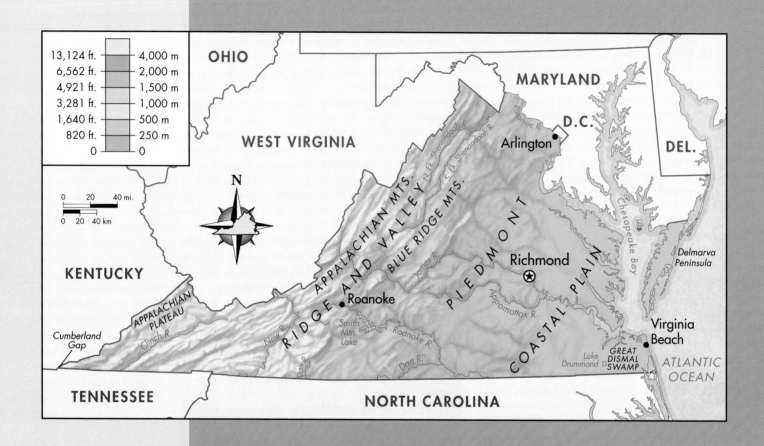

Map of Virginia and surrounding areas.

Elevation scale:

13,124 ft.	4,000 m
6,562 ft.	2,000 m
4,921 ft.	1,500 m
3,281 ft.	1,000 m
1,640 ft.	500 m
820 ft.	250 m
0	0

0   20   40 mi.

0   20   40 km

N

OHIO

WEST VIRGINIA

MARYLAND

D.C.

DEL.

Arlington

KENTUCKY

Potomac R.

N. Fk. Shenandoah R.

S. Fk. Shenandoah R.

APPALACHIAN MTS.

BLUE RIDGE MTS.

RIDGE AND VALLEY

APPALACHIAN PLATEAU

Cumberland Gap

Clinch R.

New R.

Dan R.

Smith Mtn. Lake

James R.

Roanoke

PIEDMONT

Richmond

Appomattox R.

Roanoke R.

Dan R.

COASTAL PLAIN

Chesapeake Bay

Delmarva Peninsula

Virginia Beach

Lake Drummond

GREAT DISMAL SWAMP

ATLANTIC OCEAN

TENNESSEE

NORTH CAROLINA

BLUE RIDGE MOUNTAINS

The eastern range of the Appalachian Mountains is called the Blue Ridge Mountains. The Blue Ridge Mountains were given this name because they look blue when viewed from a distance. The mountains in this region rise over 3,000 ft (914 m) above sea level. The highest peak in Virginia is Mount Rogers, at 5,729 ft (1,746 m).

The Blue Ridge is a major recreation area. The mountains are a great place for outdoor activities, including hiking, biking, and horseback riding. One of the highlights of this area is the Blue Ridge Parkway, a 469-mile (755-km) scenic road that starts in North Carolina and runs into Virginia.

Crabtree Falls in the Blue Ridge Mountains has five cascades and a vertical drop that totals 1,500 ft (457 m).

THE RIDGE AND VALLEY

The Ridge and Valley lies to the west of the Blue Ridge Mountains. A ridge is a line of hills and mountains, and a valley is an area of low, flat land between the mountains.

The Allegheny Mountains lie to the west of the Blue Ridge. In between is the Great Valley. This valley includes a famous smaller valley called the Shenandoah. Rivers in this part of Virginia are the New, Shenandoah, and Clinch.

The biggest city in the Ridge and Valley region is Roanoke. Other towns in the Ridge and Valley region are Winchester, Salem, Staunton, and Abingdon.

FIND OUT MORE

Most towers and bridges are manmade, but some in Virginia were created entirely by nature. Both the Natural Chimneys (120 ft or 37 m high) and Natural Bridge (90 ft or 27 m long) were formed from stone. What forces of nature do you think caused the Natural Chimneys and Natural Bridge to form?

APPALACHIAN PLATEAU

Located west of the Ridge and Valley region is the Appalachian Plateau, also called the Cumberland Plateau. This region covers the southwestern part of Virginia. A plateau is an elevated, but level, part of the earth's surface. Streams have made impressions on the land, creating deep ravines and winding ridges. The Plateau region is rich in mineral resources such as coal, natural gas, and petroleum.

The Cumberland Gap is located in the western tip of Virginia. A gap is a natural pass through a mountain range. The Cumberland Gap is the largest and best-known mountain gap. It was used by thousands of settlers and soldiers traveling from east to west through the Appalachian Mountains.

Beach ball sculptures at Virginia Beach can be just as much fun as real ones!

CLIMATE

Virginia's climate is warm and moist. This kind of climate is called humid subtropical. The summertime temperature often reaches 90° Fahrenheit (32° Celsius) or higher. Even so, snow usually falls throughout Virginia in the winter. Most of the state gets between 38 and 44 inches (97 to 112 centimeters) of precipitation, mostly rain, each year.

The temperatures in the mountains are lower than in the rest of Virginia. Average temperatures in the mountains range from 78° F (26° C) in the summer to about 30° F (about -1° C) in the winter. In the mountains, more than a foot of snow may fall. In the Piedmont and Tidewater regions, the average temperatures are higher.

CHAPTER THREE

VIRGINIA THROUGH HISTORY

Paleo Indians arrived in North America about 10,000 years ago. They were nomadic people who followed herds of mastodons, hunting them for food. About 3,000 years ago, natives called Woodland People lived in the area. They set up village settlements and planted corn, beans, and squash.

By 1600, there were about 20,000 Native Americans in what is now Virginia. In the west were the Cherokee people. In the east lived the Pamunkey, Mattaponi, and Powhatan. In between lived the Monacan and Manahoac. These groups spoke different languages.

The people in the Tidewater were part of a family of Native American groups called Algonquians. They made clothing and moccasins from animal furs and skins, and built dome-shaped houses made of saplings that were tied together and covered with tree bark or animal hides.

Two important Civil War battles took place on this field overlooking Bull Run. The site is now preserved as Manassas National Battlefield Park.

13

Native Americans fished off Virginia's shores.

Native people took advantage of their environment. They fished and gathered wild berries, nuts, oysters, and clams. They grew corn, beans, pumpkins, squash, and melons. The forests were full of deer, bears, elks, turkeys, and bison.

Many Algonquian tribes united in order to better protect themselves during war against other tribes. Together they formed the Powhatan Chiefdom and made Powhatan their chief.

WHO'S WHO IN VIRGINIA?

John Smith (1580-1631) was one of the founders of Jamestown. After an attack by the Algonquian Indians, Smith was captured and brought to Chief Powhatan. Smith believed that the chief's daughter, Pocahontas, saved his life. He was later released in friendship and returned to Jamestown.

JAMESTOWN

In 1604 a group of Englishmen called the Virginia Company obtained a charter, or official permission, from England's King James I to settle in the New World. In late 1606, 104 Virginia Company settlers and 40 crew members set sail for the New World.

After five months at sea, the small group arrived in the New World and chose a place to live. They stopped along a river they named after King James and built a fort in May 1607. They chose this area because it had a good harbor and land that was rich in natural resources.

A soldier, Captain John Smith, was one of the people appointed to help govern the new colony. These early settlers were not farmers, and

The first settlers at Jamestown hoped to find gold and make their fortunes.

few of them knew how to grow food. Smith explored the area around Jamestown and traded with the Powhatans for food. His resourcefulness helped the colony to survive.

The winter of 1609 was very hard for the Jamestown colonists. Supplies did not arrive, but more settlers did. Food became scarce. Many colonists died of disease and starvation. Of the 500 people at Jamestown that winter, only 60 were still alive the next spring. This period is called the "starving time." That spring, the settlers were ready to sail back to England just as the supply ships arrived.

The ships also brought a settler named John Rolfe. Rolfe brought seeds for a kind of tobacco that was unknown in Virginia. The tobacco grew well there, and in 1614, Rolfe shipped some of this new tobacco to England, making a good profit. Soon everyone was growing tobacco. Thanks to "the golden weed," the colony could now survive and even grow rich. Tobacco was so valuable in Virginia, and money so scarce, that colonists sometimes used tobacco as money.

Jamestown settlers shipped barrels of tobacco to England, which helped the new colony to support itself.

The year 1619 was very important in Virginia. That year, the first Africans arrived, as well as the first bride ship full of women who would start families. Also, the first assembly met in Jamestown that year.

The women's arrival changed the town. Now men could get married, settle on large farms called plantations, and raise families. This meant more land was being used for settlers' farms, which angered the Native Americans living there.

Tobacco farmers needed a lot of help to raise their crops. More plantations meant that settlers needed more people to work for them. To get help, plantation owners began using indentured servants. These servants agreed to work for a master, the person who paid their cost of travel to the New World, for a certain period of time. After working for about seven years, the servants were set free. The first twenty Africans to arrive in North America in 1619 were indentured servants.

As more people arrived, the Virginia Company needed a better way to govern the colony. In 1619, the first assembly, called the House of Burgesses, met in Jamestown. The assembly was made up of a governor, his council, and two citizens, called burgesses, elected from each plantation. The burgesses could pass laws, if the governor and his council approved them.

In 1622 Powhatan died, and his brother Opechancanough became chief. Opechancanough was not friendly with the Europeans. That year, Native Americans killed over three hundred settlers, and several hundred more died during the winter because of starvation and plague. The survivors wanted revenge. They attacked Native Americans without regard to whether they had participated in the violence.

King James took matters into his own hands. He revoked the Virginia Company's charter in 1624. Now Virginia was a royal colony, under England's rule. The governor of the colony would be appointed not by the Virginia Company, but by the king. The General Assembly continued to meet and pass laws.

TIMES OF CHANGE

The 1660s and 1670s were a time of great change. In 1661, the General Assembly passed a law that made lifetime slavery legal. Now African servants were slaves for life. Plantation owners saved money by using slaves instead of indentured servants.

In the early 1670s, settlers began to explore west, toward the Blue Ridge Mountains. This angered the Susquehannocks, a Native American group. They lived on this land and believed it was rightfully theirs. They began to attack the settlers. Governor William Berkeley avoided a war by coming to a peace agreement with the Susquehannocks.

Many farmers, however, believed they had a right to more land, and were angry with Governor Berkeley. In 1676, Nathaniel Bacon led a group of farmers eastward,

FIND OUT MORE

Some historians view Bacon's rebellion as a step toward democracy. Democracy is a form of government in which power is held by the people, but carried out by elected representatives. What makes our government today a democracy?

Many plantations had separate, small homes for the slaves who worked there.

where they burned Jamestown. Later that year, Bacon fell ill and died, and Bacon's rebellion collapsed. Those who took part were arrested and many were hanged.

In 1698 Jamestown suffered another fire. Instead of rebuilding the statehouse, the Governor decided to move the capital to Middle Plantation, a growing town nearby. In 1699, it was renamed Williamsburg, after King William III. Williamsburg was officially the new capital of Virginia.

In 1700, there were 63,000 people in Virginia, and the number was growing larger still. As the population grew, so did the wealth. Plantation owners needed help, so more Africans were brought to Virginia as slaves. The General Assembly began to pass rules called slave codes. The first slave code in 1705 declared that the children of enslaved people would also be slaves. By 1740, more than half of Virginia's 200,000 people were slaves.

Slaves were bought and sold by plantation owners at town auctions.

Virginians wanted more land to settle. In 1716, Governor Alexander Spotswood led an expedition to explore the land between the Blue Ridge and the Allegheny Mountains. The expedition mapped out much of Virginia's unknown territory. After the expedition, immigrants from Scotland, Ireland, and Germany began settling in the rich farmland of the Shenandoah Valley.

THE AMERICAN REVOLUTION

England wasn't the only country to settle in parts of North America. The French, who were also British rivals, claimed more and more land.

In the mid-1700s, France and England fought a war over land disputes. In the end, Britain won claim to all of North America east of the Mississippi, except for New Orleans. The war was called the French and Indian War (1754–1763), after the British colonists' enemies and their Native American allies. Sometimes it is also called the Seven Years' War.

The cost of the war—both in men and dollars—was very high. To help pay for it, the English government taxed the colonists, beginning with the Stamp Act in 1765. It required colonists to pay a tax on every piece of printed paper they used. The colonists protested and the Stamp Act was repealed, but England later passed taxes on tea and other goods. All the colonies, including Virginia, were disgusted by the taxes.

In 1774, leaders from twelve colonies came to the First Continental Congress in Philadelphia to discuss what to do. Patrick Henry, George Washington, and Richard Henry Lee served as Virginia's delegates, or representatives, at this meeting. Peyton Randolph, another Virginian, was president. At the time, it was decided that they were not yet ready to declare independence from England.

The Second Continental Congress met in Philadelphia in 1775. By then, British soldiers and

WHAT'S IN A NAME?

What are the origins of some Virginia names?

Name	Comes from or means
Appomattox	Named after the Appomattock tribe
Shenandoah	Shenando, meaning "daughter of the stars"
Chincoteague	Algonquian word meaning "beautiful land over the water"
Newport News	Named for Captain Christopher Newport, who brought the first settlers to Jamestown
Nottoway	Nadowa tribe; "nadowa" means "snake" or "enemy"
Pocahontas	"Playful one"
Poquoson	"Pocosin," an Algonquian word meaning "dismal" or "swamp"
Roanoke	"Rawrenock," the shell beads worn by natives and used as trade goods

WHO'S WHO IN VIRGINIA?

George Washington (1732–1799) fought in the French and Indian War before becoming the commander of the American army. He was unanimously elected the first president of the United States in 1789, and was re-elected in 1793. Washington is often called the "Father of Our Country."

colonists had already clashed at Lexington and Concord in Massachusetts. George Washington was appointed to command an army and the American Revolution (1775–1783) began.

Although the war raged on, Virginia declared itself to be independent of England in June 1776, when it adopted a state constitution, a document that outlines rules and a form of government. Part of the constitution was a Declaration of Rights, written by George Mason. This section outlined citizens' rights and set limits to what the government could do.

Virginia played the largest role of any of the colonies in forming the United States. Virginian George Washington led the American army against the British. On July 4, 1776, seven Virginians signed the Declaration of Independence, a document that announced the separation of the colonies from England. Thomas Jefferson was chosen to write the Declaration because of his excellent writing ability and also because he was a representative of the largest colony, Virginia.

American soldiers fought the Revolutionary War for six and a half years. On October 19, 1781, General Washington accepted the surrender of British General Lord Charles Cornwallis at Yorktown. Yorktown was the last major battle of the Revolutionary War. The Treaty of Paris formally recognized the new nation in 1783.

British troops surrendered at the Battle of Yorktown, the last battle of the Revolutionary War.

THE U.S. CONSTITUTION

At first, the thirteen colonies united under a document called the Articles of Confederation. The Articles formed a weak government that worked poorly. In 1787, the Constitutional Convention met to form a new government. George Washington was president of this convention. The delegates wrote the United States Constitution.

If nine of the thirteen colonies ratified, or accepted, the Constitution, it would become law. The first colony to ratify it was Delaware. Virginia, however, refused to accept the Constitution until a Bill of Rights was added. The Bill would specify the rights of every citizen of the United States. Virginia's Declaration of Rights served as a model for the Bill of Rights, as did Virginia's Statute for Religious Freedom, a law that sepa-

James Madison is the "father of the Constitution."

rated church and state. When the Bill of Rights was added, Virginia became the tenth state to ratify the Constitution on June 25, 1788.

Four of the country's first five presidents were Virginians. During Thomas Jefferson's term, the United States purchased a large amount of land from France. From the Mississippi River in the east to the Rocky Mountains in the west, the Louisiana Purchase was one of the biggest land purchases in history. The country nearly doubled in size. Jefferson sent two Virginians, Meriwether Lewis and William Clark, to explore the new territory.

James Madison was the country's fourth president, from 1809–1817. Madison became known as the "father of the Constitution" for his work at the Constitutional Convention and afterwards. James Monroe was the fifth president, from 1817–1825. He issued the Monroe Doctrine. This document declared that European governments must not interfere in North or South America.

John Marshall, another Virginian, was chief justice of the U.S. Supreme Court for 34 years. Presidents William Henry Harrison, and John Tyler were also Virginians.

SLAVERY AND THE CIVIL WAR

Although the country was now united, not everyone had the same idea of what the United States should be. A major source of disagreement was slavery. By the 1830s, the only states that allowed slavery were in the South. Although many leaders believed slavery should end, many also owned slaves themselves. The economy of the southern states depended on slavery. In the North, most people worked in factories and businesses where they were paid wages. Northern and Southern people led very different lives.

Nat Turner led a slave rebellion in hopes of starting a black nation in Virginia. Ultimately, his plan failed, and Turner was hanged.

In some parts of the South there were more enslaved African-Americans than whites. Many southern whites feared an uprising. In 1831 Nat Turner, a slave in Virginia, led such an uprising. His followers killed over fifty white people, but the rebellion failed to gain freedom for slaves. Instead, more strict treatment of African-Americans resulted. African-American preachers were not allowed to speak in churches, in case they told slaves to revolt. Slaves were not allowed to read and write. Those who disobeyed were harshly punished.

In 1859, abolitionist John Brown and a few followers attacked a warehouse of weapons in Harpers Ferry (now in West Virginia). He strongly believed that slavery must end immediately. Brown wanted to give the weapons to local slaves, believing they would fight for their freedom. Brown's scheme failed, and he was hanged.

President Abraham Lincoln, elected in 1860, did not want slavery to spread into the west. Many southern states felt so strongly about slavery that they seceded, or withdrew, from the United States. Leaders in these states felt strongly that states should have the right to decide for themselves if slavery should be allowed. Together they formed their own country, called the Confederate States of America. In May 1861 Richmond became the Confederacy's capital.

In April 1861, the Civil War (1861–1865) began in South Carolina. President Lincoln asked General Robert E. Lee, a Virginian, to command the Union Army. Lee refused, and instead commanded the Confederate forces of Northern Virginia. The Civil War raged for four bloody years, and Virginia bore the brunt of the fighting.

Over half of the Civil War's 4,000 battles took place in Virginia. The first major battle, Bull Run (also called Manassas), was fought near Washington, D.C. The Confederacy won the battles of Fredericksburg and Chancellorsville. Western Virginia, particularly the rich farmland of the Shenandoah Valley, was also the scene of much fighting.

The city of Richmond suffered greatly as a result of the Civil War. This drawing shows the city in the midst of battle on April 2, 1865.

The historic meeting between General Lee and General Grant ended the southern states' attempt to create a separate nation.

After Union General Ulysses S. Grant defeated General Lee at Petersburg, near Richmond, the war was nearly over. Here, General Lee surrendered to General Grant at Appomattox Courthouse on April 9, 1865.

RECONSTRUCTION AND GROWTH

After the Civil War, the South was devastated, especially Virginia. Four years of fighting and scavenging by soldiers had destroyed farms and railroads. Slave labor was gone, plantations were broken up, and the state's economy was shattered. Virginia was put under military rule, because its government simply could not function. Virginia officially rejoined the Union on January 26, 1870.

Virginia was in ruins after the Civil War. In the years that followed, called Reconstruction, many industries and businesses had to be rebuilt.

Newly freed slaves had little food, clothing, or education. The Freedmen's Bureau, a federal agency, assisted former slaves in getting an education and finding jobs. Many former slaves became sharecroppers.

Conditions for African-Americans improved right after the Civil War. In 1869, Virginia adopted a new constitution that recognized the right of African-American men to vote. Despite that, however, African-Americans were still not treated as equal. Over the next thirty years, Virginia and other states passed laws of segregation, requiring African-Americans

FIND OUT MORE

Sharecroppers did not own the land they farmed. They shared their crops with the owner. The owners charged them for the use of tools and seeds. Why do you think this system kept sharecroppers from growing rich?

Segregation affected every part of daily life. The Old Dominion Railroad Station in Rosslyn had two separate entrances to the waiting room—the door on the right is marked "Colored."

to be separate from whites. They had to sit in different areas in buses and trains, go to different churches and schools, and even use different water fountains and bathrooms.

The poll tax was another form of discrimination against African-Americans. In 1902 it became necessary to pay a special tax in order to vote. Since most African-Americans were poor, they could not pay the tax and so were not allowed to vote. Laws that allowed such discrimination were called Jim Crow laws.

After the Civil War, many people left rural areas to seek jobs in cities. In the 1880s, coal had been discovered in western Virginia. Roanoke became a bustling railroad terminal and grew into a city. Newport News became an important shipbuilding center.

Virginia's economy grew stronger, especially during World War I (1914–1918). About 100,000 Virginians joined the armed forces during the war. New factories and military training centers in Virginia helped the state prosper.

But discrimination and violence against African-Americans continued. More than one hundred African-Americans in Virginia were lynched, or killed by mobs, between 1880 and 1920. The terrorists were almost never arrested or punished. Thousands of African-Americans left the South. It was not until 1928 that Virginia outlawed lynching.

The Great Depression occurred in the 1930s. The stock market crashed and the United States was plunged into a terrible economic time. Many businesses shut down. Jobs were scarce and people had little money. To create more jobs, President Franklin D. Roosevelt started programs that employed people to build parks and public buildings. The Norfolk Botanical Gardens and the Virginia State Library were built. Other government projects brought electricity to rural Virginia. The start of World War II in 1939 helped end the Great Depression.

The United States entered World War II (1939–1945) in 1941. Virginia's industries—coal production and shipbuilding—were very important to the nation during the war. New industries, like chemicals,

FAMOUS FIRSTS

- The first theater in the U.S. was built at Williamsburg in 1716
- World's first ironclad ships, U.S.S. *Monitor* and C.S.S. *Virginia*, battled in Hampton Roads in 1862
- The military song "Taps" was first played in 1862 at Berkeley Plantation
- Virginian Maggie Lena Walker was the first woman and African-American bank president in the country
- The first American astronauts were trained at NASA Langley Research Center in Hampton
- Virginian L. Douglas Wilder became the first elected African-American governor in the U.S. in 1989

The Pentagon is one of the world's largest office buildings. It has 23,000 employees, 131 stairways, and offices that cover 3,705,793 sq ft (344,279 sq m).

electronics, and weapons, brought an economic boom. In 1943, the U.S. Department of Defense opened its headquarters, the Pentagon, in northern Virginia. About three hundred thousand Virginians fought in Europe during World War II.

THE CIVIL RIGHTS MOVEMENT

In 1954, the U.S. Supreme Court ruled that segregation in public schools was unconstitutional and worked against the basic beliefs of the constitution. This decision launched several years of struggle. Some lawmakers wanted to keep different races separate. Others favored putting an end to racial separation, or desegregation.

In Virginia, state leaders closed public schools and opened private ones to resist desegregation. This practice was called "massive resistance." Soon, many public schools had large African-American populations and few whites. Nevertheless, desegregation came to Virginia schools beginning in 1959.

In the 1960s, African-Americans staged sit-ins, bus boycotts, and other protests to draw attention to unfair laws. Sit-ins began after a five-and-dime store in North Carolina refused to seat and serve African-Americans at a whites-only lunch counter. This led to protesters sitting at lunch counters all over the country as a way of speaking out against segregation. Another form of protest were the bus boycotts, when thousands of African-Americans stopped using buses, rather than sit in the blacks-only section.

As the racial climate changed, Virginia reached several milestones. In 1964, the poll tax was abolished. In 1969, an African-American, L. Douglas Wilder, was elected a state senator.

During and after the civil rights movement, life in Virginia changed for ordinary African-Americans. No longer were there separate drinking fountains and restrooms, or separate seats in public buildings. African-

American mayors were elected in Virginia cities, beginning with Petersburg in 1984. In 1989, L. Douglas Wilder became the first elected African-American governor in the United States.

INDUSTRIAL CHANGE

Virginia's economy also changed after the 1950s. Fishing and coal mining increased production. Dairy and beef farming, lumber and paper milling, and service industries (companies that sell services rather than goods) grew most rapidly. Manufacturing also increased.

Because of the growth of industry in the 1960s and 1970s, Virginia's air and waterways became polluted. The government passed laws in the 1970s and 1980s requiring clean air and water. Big factories could no longer dump waste in rivers, or pollute the air with harmful smoke. Ordinary Virginians are also more aware of the environment. For example, many communities now recycle their waste.

Pollution from farming and industry has caused the number of fish and shellfish in the Chesapeake Bay to decline. Both the state and private groups are working to help save the Bay. Still, fewer Virginians will be fishermen in the future.

Coal production in western Virginia has dropped since 1990. Coal and oil pollute the air, and will eventually run out. Many scientists believe Americans must turn to

FIND OUT MORE

Virginia isn't the only state concerned about pollution. As a matter of fact, countries all over the world are trying to cut down on pollution of all kinds. Air pollution is one of the biggest problems, and often it is invisible. How does air become polluted? What kinds of things can cause air pollution?

other forms of energy, such as solar and wind power. These sources of energy are clean, and will never run out.

Also in danger in the 1990s was Virginia's historic ground. In 1998, the National Trust for Historic Preservation announced that Chancellorsville battlefield was in danger. Too many people and businesses were buying land on all sides of the battlefield. Two years later, federal funds and private groups had saved the battlefield.

This plaque marks historic ground in front of Peers House at Appomattox. It commemorates the place of the formal surrender ceremony of the Civil War.

Virginians try to keep their state beautiful by preserving historic sites and the environment. They also try to make society better by fighting racism and poverty. In the new millennium, Virginians will continue to learn from the past and look toward the future.

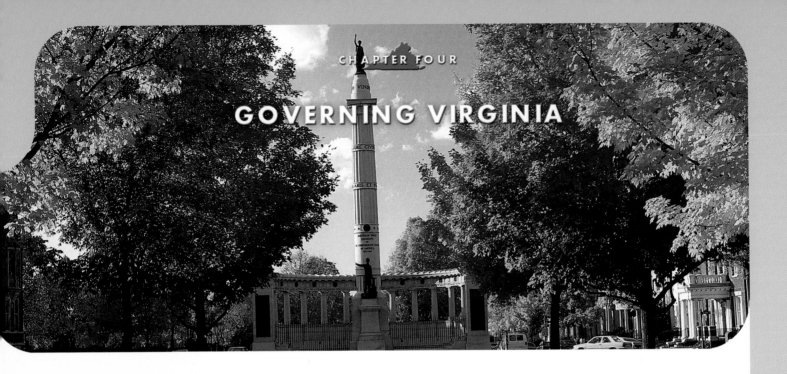

CHAPTER FOUR

GOVERNING VIRGINIA

Six monuments and many historic homes line Richmond's Monument Avenue, often called the most beautiful boulevard in the South.

Virginia's first state government was established in 1776, when the constitution was adopted. The constitution is a document that lays out the laws and principles governing the state. Since then, the state constitution has been amended, or revised, five times, but much of the document remains true to the original version. Some changes have given more power to state government. Other changes have recognized the civil rights of more people.

Virginia is a commonwealth. The word *commonwealth* means the welfare of a community of people. Only three other states in the country are known as commonwealths—Kentucky, Pennsylvania, and Massachusetts. Virginians strongly believe that their state government exists for the good of its citizens. Like the federal government, Virginia's government has three branches: the legislative, executive, and judicial.

This picture shows a statue of George Washington and the American flag in Virginia.

THE LEGISLATIVE BRANCH

The legislative branch creates and changes the state's laws. Virginia's legislative branch is called the General Assembly. It is made up of two groups: the Senate and the House of Delegates. Senators and delegates meet with people throughout the state to get ideas for new laws. A new law that is being introduced is called a bill.

FIND OUT MORE

Virginia's General Assembly is the oldest law-making body in all of North and South America. It is the job of the members of the General Assembly to decide whether a bill—an idea for a new law—should become official. How does a bill become a law?

There are 40 senators and 100 delegates. They are elected every other year. Senators serve for four years, and delegates for two. The General Assembly meets in the capitol building in Richmond for either 30 or 60 days a year.

THE EXECUTIVE BRANCH

The executive branch enforces and carries out the laws of Virginia. The chief officer of this branch is the governor. He or she is elected by the people of Virginia. The governor serves one four-year term. The governor appoints people to state offices and can sign bills into law, or veto (reject) them. Also elected is a lieutenant governor and an attorney general.

THE JUDICIAL BRANCH

The third branch is the judicial branch. This branch interprets the laws and resolves disputes. These duties are carried out through the court system.

There are 122 lower courts in 31 sections called circuit courts. The General Assembly chooses judges for these courts, who serve for eight years. Circuit courts hear criminal cases and civil cases, or private disputes between two or more parties. All circuit court cases require a jury, or groups of citizens that listen to both sides of the dispute and make a decision as to the outcome of a case.

VIRGINIA GOVERNORS

Name	Term	Name	Term
Patrick Henry	1776–1779	Henry A. Wise	1856–1860
Thomas Jefferson	1779–1781	John Letcher	1860–1864
William Fleming	1781	William Smith	1864–1865
Thomas Nelson, Jr.	1781	Francis H. Pierpont	1865–1868
Benjamin Harrison	1781–1784	Henry H. Wells	1868–1869
Patrick Henry	1784–1786	Gilbert C. Walker	1869–1874
Edmund Randolph	1786–1788	James L. Kemper	1874–1878
Beverley Randolph	1788–1791	Frederick W. M. Holliday	1878–1882
Henry Lee	1791–1794	William Evelyn Cameron	1882–1886
Robert Brooke	1794–1796	Fitzhugh Lee	1886–1890
James Wood	1796–1799	Philip W. McKinney	1890–1894
Hardin Burnley	1799	Charles T. O'Ferrall	1894–1898
J. Pendleton	1799	James H. Tyler	1898–1902
James Monroe	1799–1802	Andrew Jackson Montague	1902–1906
John Page	1802–1805	Claude A. Swanson	1906–1910
William H. Cabell	1805–1808	William Hodges Mann	1910–1914
John Tyler, Sr.	1808–1811	Henry Carter Stuart	1914–1918
George W. Smith	1811	Westmoreland Davis	1918–1922
James Monroe	1811	Elbert Lee Trinkle	1922–1926
Peyton Randolph	1811–1812	Harry Flood Byrd	1926–1930
James Barbour	1812–1814	John G. Pollard	1930–1934
Wilson Cary Nicholas	1814–1816	George C. Peery	1934–1938
James Patton Preston	1816–1819	James H. Price	1938–1942
Thomas Mann Randolph	1819–1822	Colgate W. Darden, Jr.	1942–1946
James Pleasants	1822–1825	William M. Tuck	1946–1950
John Tyler, Jr.	1825–1827	John S. Battle	1950–1954
William B. Giles	1827–1830	Thomas B. Stanley	1954–1958
John Floyd	1830–1834	J. Lindsay Almond, Jr.	1958–1962
Littleton Waller Tazewell	1834–1836	Albertis S. Harrison, Jr.	1962–1966
Wyndham Robertson	1836–1837	Mills E. Godwin, Jr.	1966–1970
David Campbell	1837–1840	A. Linwood Holton, Jr.	1970–1974
Thomas W. Gilmer	1840–1841	Mills E. Godwin, Jr.	1974–1978
John M. Patton	1841	John N. Dalton	1978–1982
John Rutherford	1841–1842	Charles S. Robb	1982–1986
John Munford Gregory	1842–1843	Gerald Baliles	1986–1990
James McDowell	1843–1846	L. Douglas Wilder	1990–1994
William Smith	1846–1849	George Allen	1994–1998
John Buchanan Floyd	1849–1852	James S. Gilmore III	1998–
Joseph Johnson	1852–1856		

VIRGINIA STATE GOVERNMENT

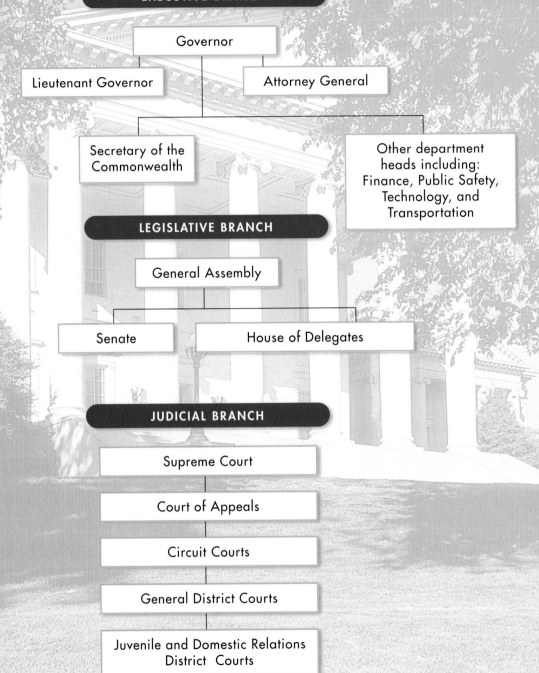

EXECUTIVE BRANCH

Governor

Lieutenant Governor

Attorney General

Secretary of the Commonwealth

Other department heads including: Finance, Public Safety, Technology, and Transportation

LEGISLATIVE BRANCH

General Assembly

Senate

House of Delegates

JUDICIAL BRANCH

Supreme Court

Court of Appeals

Circuit Courts

General District Courts

Juvenile and Domestic Relations District Courts

The General District Court hears cases involving traffic offenses and misdemeanors (small crimes), but there is no jury involved. A judge hears each case and makes the decision on his own.

If someone is unhappy with the outcome of their case, they can go to the Court of Appeals. The Court of Appeals reviews lower court decisions. The Supreme Court of Virginia also reviews lower court decisions and helps to develop the state's laws. Seven members serve on the Supreme Court for twelve years. Members are chosen by the General Assembly.

The Virginia state capitol building also served as the capitol for the Confederate States of America.

TAKE A TOUR OF RICHMOND, THE CAPITAL

Virginia has had three capitals. The first was Jamestown. In 1699, Williamsburg became the capital. In 1779, America was at war with Britain, and Williamsburg was too easy to capture. As a result, in 1780 the capital moved further inland, to Richmond. Thomas Jefferson designed the first permanent capitol building there.

During the Civil War, Richmond was the capital of the Confederate States of America. In 1865, the city was captured, and

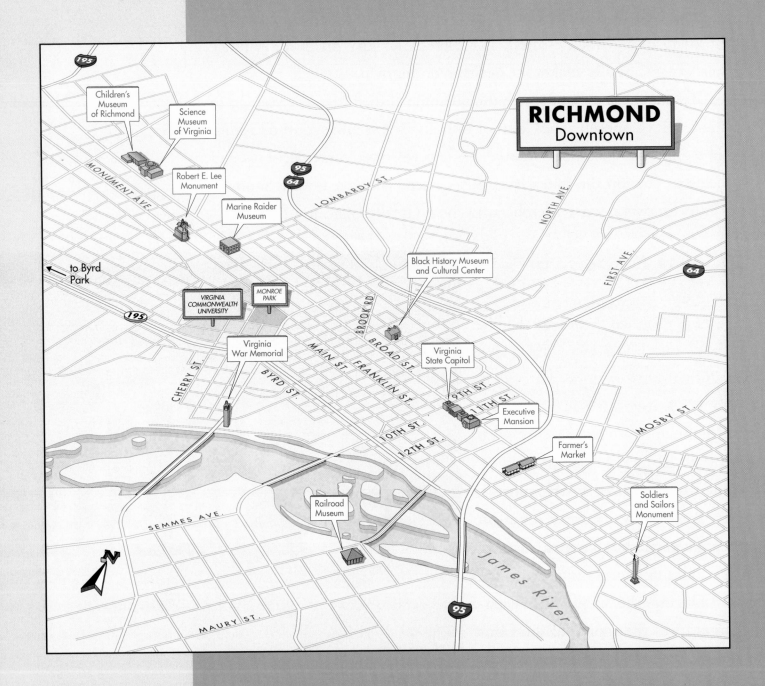

RICHMOND
Downtown

Children's Museum of Richmond

Science Museum of Virginia

Robert E. Lee Monument

Marine Raider Museum

MONUMENT AVE.

LOMBARDY ST.

NORTH AVE.

FIRST AVE.

to Byrd Park

Black History Museum and Cultural Center

VIRGINIA COMMONWEALTH UNIVERSITY

MONROE PARK

BROOK RD.

Virginia War Memorial

CHERRY ST.

BYRD ST.

MAIN ST.

BROAD ST.

FRANKLIN ST.

Virginia State Capitol

9TH ST.

11TH ST.

Executive Mansion

10TH ST.

12TH ST.

MOSBY ST.

Farmer's Market

Railroad Museum

SEMMES AVE.

James River

Soldiers and Sailors Monument

MAURY ST.

much of it burned. Richmond was rebuilt, and today it is very different from the Richmond of the 1860s.

The Executive Mansion, where Virginia's governors live, is the oldest continuously occupied governor's mansion in the United States. It was first used in 1813. Near this building is the White House of the Confederacy. This is where Confederate president Jefferson Davis lived with

The Executive Mansion in Virginia has been home to governors and their families since 1813.

his family during the Civil War. Nearby is the Museum of the Confederacy. It has the world's largest collection of Confederate artifacts. The Richmond Riverfront and Canal Walk is an exciting, new way to learn about Richmond's past. You can walk alongside the James River or take a boat tour down the canal, where important places from the city's past are marked.

Even though Richmond is full of history, there's plenty that's modern. The Science Museum of Virginia has exhibits that people can touch and examine to learn about scientific ideas. And you can't get much more modern than race cars! The Richmond International Raceway attracts lots of sports fans. Richmond is a thriving capital city full of industry, shops, and parks, as well as historical attractions.

NASCAR driver Jeff Burton holds a trophy at Richmond's International Raceway.

CHAPTER FIVE

THE PEOPLE AND PLACES OF VIRGINIA

The people of Virginia represent a variety of backgrounds. Almost eight out of every ten Virginians are of European descent. Soon after the first English settlers came, people from Germany, Wales, France, Ireland, and Scotland arrived. There was also the unwilling immigration of millions of Africans. Today, about two out of ten Virginians are of African descent.

In the twentieth century, immigrants began to arrive from other places, such as Latin America and Asia. Now, about five of every 100 Virginians are of Asian or Hispanic descent. A very small number of Native Americans still live in Virginia. On the Middle Peninsula in the Tidewater region are two reservations, the Pamunkey and Mattaponi. They are the oldest reservations in the country.

Religion has always been important to Virginians. The first European settlers were almost all Anglican (Episcopal)—that is, members of

Richmond is a big, bustling city blended with a taste of history.

Lee Chapel at Washington and Lee University in Lexington attracts over 50,000 visitors each year.

the Church of England. Until 1786, Anglicanism was Virginia's official religion. Today, Virginia has many other Protestant Christians, like Baptists and Methodists, as well as a large number of Roman Catholics. Many Jewish people call Virginia home, particularly in Richmond and other eastern cities.

Rollerblading is a popular activity on the Virginia Beach boardwalk.

WORKING IN VIRGINIA

About a third of Virginians today work in service industries, such as banking, real estate, sales, and tourism. Tourism brings much money to Virginia. In the 1990s, tourists spent about ten billion dollars a year in the state!

Many people in Virginia work for the government. The Norfolk Naval Station and Shipyard is the largest in the country. Thousands of people work at nearby NASA-Langley Research Center, doing research to improve the performance of air and spacecraft. In northern Virginia,

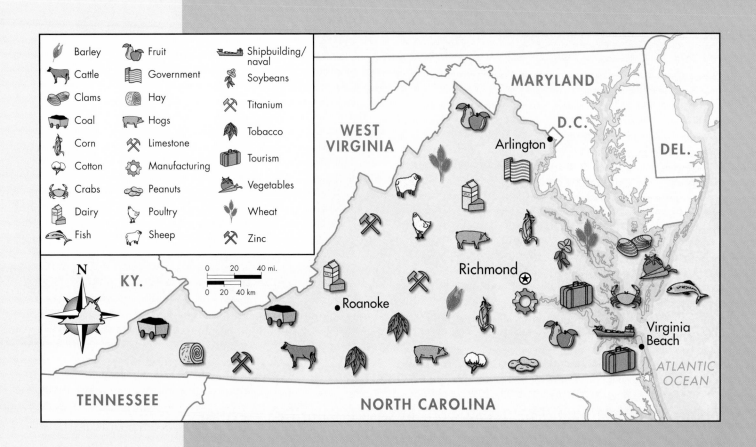

Barley	Fruit	Shipbuilding/naval
Cattle	Government	Soybeans
Clams	Hay	Titanium
Coal	Hogs	Tobacco
Corn	Limestone	Tourism
Cotton	Manufacturing	Vegetables
Crabs	Peanuts	Wheat
Dairy	Poultry	Zinc
Fish	Sheep	

N

KY.

0   20   40 mi.
0   20   40 km

WEST VIRGINIA

MARYLAND

D.C.

DEL.

Arlington

Richmond

Roanoke

Virginia Beach

ATLANTIC OCEAN

TENNESSEE

NORTH CAROLINA

many people work for the government at the Pentagon and at the Marine Corps base at Quantico.

Some important industries in Virginia are fishing, food processing, textile and clothing manufacturing, chemicals, lumber and paper, furniture, and ships. Also, northern Virginia has more than a thousand companies that make electronics and communications equipment.

Norfolk Southern Corporation operates the Norfolk Southern Railway. This company began by building a railroad between Hopewell and Richmond in 1838.

In Richmond, several large companies employ thousands of Virginians. Circuit City is a chain of electronics stores. Motorola makes communications equipment. Phillip Morris manufactures cigarettes, and James River Corporation makes paper products such as Dixie cups.

In northern Virginia, the Gannett Company in Arlington publishes *USA Today*, a national daily newspaper. In McLean, Mars Incorporated makes candy bars, like M&M's and Snickers bars. In Dulles, America Online provides entertainment and news to millions of people through the Internet.

NASA-Langley Research Center in Hampton works to improve today's aircraft and develop ideas for future aircraft.

Agriculture still produces a lot of income. Virginia is one of the top ten producers of peanuts, turkeys, and apples. Tobacco brings more than $200 million into the state every year. Beef cattle, dairy products, pork, wheat and grains, soybeans, peaches, and chickens are also important products.

Winchester, Virginia is one of the top ten apple producers in the United States.

The Chesapeake Bay has greatly influenced much of Virginia's industry. Both the Norfolk Naval Station and Shipyard and Newport News Shipbuilding in Newport News are located near the Bay and harbor. Newport News Shipbuilding is the largest privately owned shipyard in the world. Also, some commercial fishers live by the Bay and make their living by catching fish and shellfish. Virginia is the third largest seafood-producing state.

Newport News Shipbuilding has been building ships since 1891. Today it also builds aircraft carriers and submarines.

Beautiful Shenandoah Valley attracts many visitors with its great trails for hiking, biking, walking, and other outdoor activities.

Shenandoah Valley

Nestled in the Shenandoah Valley is the town of Winchester, founded in 1732. The beauty of the town and the valley has made Winchester "Virginia's wedding capital." Visit New Market Battlefield Park, where cadets from the Virginia Military Institute fought with Confederate troops to defeat the Union Army during the Civil War. You can take a tour of the battlefield and visit the military museum. The Shenandoah Apple Blossom Festival is the area's largest event. Dances, parades and band competitions attract more than 300,000 people—and celebrities—each year!

National park, forest, or recreation area
Highway
Capital city
City
Tourist site

OHIO

WEST VIRGINIA

MARYLAND

Arlington

D.C.

81

66

Quantico

Alexandria

DEL.

SHENANDOAH
N.P.

Fredericksburg

GEORGE
WASHINGTON
N.F.

Waynesboro

95

N

Charlottesville

64

0   20   40 mi.

0   20   40 km

KENTUCKY

64

Greenville

64

Williamsburg

Richmond

64

MT. ROGERS NATIONAL
RECREATION AREA

81

Roanoke

Colonial
N.H.P.

Newport News

77

Virginia
Beach

85

95

81

77

Norfolk

ATLANTIC
OCEAN

TENNESSEE

NORTH CAROLINA

You'll also find natural wonders in this area, such as spectacular caverns and strange rock formations. Every August at Natural Chimneys, a Jousting Tournament draws big crowds. Jousting is a sport in which two people on horseback try to knock each other off with long poles called lances. At this tournament, though, competitors try to capture small rings on the tips of lances.

Towering stone columns and frozen fountains are part of the spectacular rock formations—some of which are over 7 million years old—found at Luray Caverns.

In Roanoke, nicknamed "Star City," locals and tourists alike enjoy seeing the animals at Mill Mountain Zoo. At night, Mill Mountain's huge manmade star is lit with white neon lights, visible from miles away. Roanoke is also home to the Virginia Museum of Transportation, which tells about the history of railroads in Virginia.

Southwest Blue Ridge Highlands

Take a drive through the Blue Ridge Mountains, often called the most beautiful part of Virginia, on the Blue Ridge Parkway or Skyline Drive. The highlands are home to a thriving mountain culture. Visitors can lis-

The Blue Ridge Parkway is 469 miles (755 km) of road that winds its way through Virginia's southern Appalachian region.

FIND OUT MORE

The Blue Ridge Parkway runs through two states—the northern part is in Virginia, and the southern part is in North Carolina. It is a total of 469 miles (755 km) long and is almost evenly divided between both states. If you divide the parkway in half, how many miles does it run in each state?

ten to country music and enjoy folk art. You can also learn about Virginia's frontier history in Atkins' one-room schoolhouse and Settlers Museum.

Other attractions in the area include the historic Barter Theatre in Abingdon. It opened in 1933, when people could see a play for "35 cents or the equivalent in produce." Today the theater is a historical landmark. The Birthplace of Country Music Alliance Museum in Bristol is a good place to find out about Bristol's musical heritage. Hikers, bikers, and canoers can enjoy the Virginia Creeper Trail, Hungry Mother State Park, and Cumberland Gap National Park at the Kentucky border. Visitors can also explore Virginia's highest peaks, Mount Rogers and White Top Mountain.

Visitors to Cumberland Gap can stand on a mountaintop overlook and see three states at once—Virginia, Tennessee, and Kentucky.

Northern Virginia

In northern Virginia, Fredericksburg and Manassas are national Civil War battlefield parks. Visitors can tour huge plantation houses at Mount Vernon, George Washington's home, and Arlington, the home of Confederate General Robert E. Lee. During the Civil War, the grounds became a national cemetery when Union soldiers were buried there.

The Tomb of the Unknowns at Arlington National Cemetery contains the remains of unknown American soldiers from World Wars I and II, and the Korean War. The tomb is guarded 24 hours a day all year round.

Alexandria's Old Town keeps the look of an old city, even in its new buildings.

Northern Virginia has many historic towns, like Alexandria, Fairfax, Leesburg, and Warrenton. The beautiful buildings and small shops selling antiques and arts and crafts attract many visitors.

Chesapeake Bay

If you travel south to the Northern Neck Peninsula of the Chesapeake Bay, you'll find several historic plantation houses. They show how wealthy Virginians lived long ago. Inside you'll find elegant furniture, paintings, and historical artifacts. Often there are beautiful historic gardens, too.

The Middle Peninsula, south of the Northern Neck, is home to the popular Urbanna Oyster Festival. Every November, visitors and locals gobble up these local shellfish. You can also watch the experts test their speed and skill in a contest of oyster shucking, or separating the oyster from its shell.

Central Virginia

The homes of important historical figures like Patrick Henry, Thomas Jefferson, James Madison, and James Monroe are all located in central Virginia and can be toured by visitors. You'll also see plenty of Civil War sites, including national parks and museums at Petersburg, City Point, Appomattox, and of course, Richmond.

After experiencing all this history you might be ready for some action! Not far from Richmond is a popular amusement park, Paramount's Kings Dominion. Water parks, stage shows, and wild rides (like the new Hypersonic XLC roller coaster) make this a popular stop right off Interstate 95.

Peanuts came to Virginia by way of colonial traders who ate peanuts aboard ships because they were cheap and of high-food value. Today, the peanut industry makes millions of dollars for Virginia, and also North Carolina. Try the recipe below for candy-coated peanuts that will make your mouth water! Remember, ask a grownup to help you.

PEANUT CANDY

1 quart molasses
4 cups roasted, shelled peanuts
1 cup brown sugar
1/2 cup margarine

1. Combine the molasses, brown sugar, and margarine in a large pot. Simmer over low heat for thirty minutes.
2. Add peanuts and heat for fifteen minutes.
3. After the candy cools, make small cakes of the candy and place them on a lightly greased baking sheet. Let them harden. Enjoy!

During the day, no cars are permitted on Duke of Gloucester Street in Colonial Williamsburg. Stroll down the street and you'll find historic homes, taverns, and shops.

Tidewater and Hampton Roads

The "Historic Triangle" of Jamestown, Yorktown, and Williamsburg welcomes nearly a million visitors each year. No one lives at Jamestown anymore, but it is a national park. Here you can see the remains of the 1607 James fort, which was recently discovered by archaeologists. Near the park, visitors can see a reconstruction of the fort, a rebuilt Powhatan village, and replicas of the first ships to arrive at Jamestown: the *Susan Constant, Godspeed,* and *Discovery.* At the Yorktown National Battlefield

A shepherd in colonial dress tends to her sheep in Colonial Williamsburg.

and the Yorktown Victory Center, visitors can see the battlefield where Lord Cornwallis surrendered in 1781 and an army camp. "Soldiers" show visitors what life was like in General Washington's Continental army.

Along Route 5 are many large plantation houses where famous families lived, like the Harrisons, the Tylers, and the Carters. The Carters lived at Shirley Plantation, founded in 1613. Inside the mansion is a 250 year-old "flying" staircase—it has no visible

Shirley Plantation is the oldest plantation in Virginia. It housed every generation of one family for four centuries.

means of support. Beautiful historical furniture at Shirley shows you how the wealthiest Virginians lived.

Hampton Roads is home to many fine museums, like the Virginia Air and Space Museum, which has artifacts from the American space program. The Mariners' Museum in Newport News houses the U.S.S. *Monitor*,

With 38 miles (61 km) of beach, Virginia Beach is a popular vacation spot for families.

Fun fish sculptures sit just off the boardwalk.

the world's first ironclad ship. The Virginia Living Museum in Newport News showcases the animals of Virginia, while the Botanical Gardens in Norfolk displays plants and flowers.

Virginia Beach, the state's largest city, is a resort town with a large boardwalk, shops, and a fine beach. Outside of urban areas lies the Great Dismal Swamp, a wetland area and wildlife refuge.

Eastern Shore

The Eastern Shore National Wildlife Refuge offers trails to view many birds, butterflies, and other animals. The Eastern Shore is also known for its excellent seafood. Crabcakes, clams, and oysters are specialties of the Eastern Shore. The most famous part of eastern Virginia is probably the wild ponies on Assateague Island. Each July, ponies from the Virginia herd (part of the herd is in Maryland) are rounded up to swim from Assateague Island to Chincoteague. Here, an auction raises money for the town of Chincoteague and also thins the herd to make sure there is enough food and space on the island for the wild horses. People come every year to buy ponies as pets.

Virginia is filled with history, natural beauty, and friendly people. When Captain John Smith arrived with the first settlers, he called Virginia "a fruitful and delightsome land." Even today, Virginia's many residents and visitors would surely agree.

EXTRA! EXTRA!

In 1947, a writer named Marguerite Henry published a book called *Misty of Chincoteague*, about a wild pony. Henry's book became a classic and made the island and the ponies famous.

Each year some wild ponies from Chincoteague are sold to families who will take good care of them.

VIRGINIA ALMANAC

Statehood date and number: June 25, 1788/10th

State seal: adopted 1776, modified 1930

State flag: adopted in 1861

Geographic center: 5 miles SW of Buckingham, in Buckingham County

Total area/rank: 42,326 sq mi (109,624 sq km)/35th

Coastline/rank: 112 mi (180 km)/15th

Borders: West Virginia, Kentucky, Tennessee, North Carolina, Maryland, Washington, D.C., Atlantic Ocean

Highest/lowest elevation: Mount Rogers, 5,729 ft (1,746 m)/sea level

Hottest/coldest temperature: 110°F (43.3°C) at Balcony Falls on July 15, 1954/-30°F (-34.4°C) at Mtn. Lake Bio on January 22, 1985

Land area/rank: 39,598 sq mi (102,558 sq km)/37th

Inland water area: 2,728 sq mi (7,065 sq km)

Population/rank: 7,078,515/12th

Population of major cities:
Virginia Beach: 425,257
Norfolk: 234,403
Chesapeake: 199,184
Richmond: 197,790
Newport News: 180,150
Hampton: 146,437
Alexandria: 128,283
Portsmouth: 100,565
Lynchburg: 65,269
Suffolk: 63,677

Origin of state name: After Queen Elizabeth I of England, who was called "the Virgin Queen"

State capital: Richmond

Counties: 95

State government: 40 senators, 100 delegates

Major rivers, lakes: Potomac, Rappahannock, York, James, New, Elizabeth, Nottoway, Rapidan, Roanoke, Shenandoah, Anna, Appomattox, Clinch, Dan Rivers; Lake Anna, Smith Mountain Lake

Farm products: Tobacco, grain, corn, soybeans, peanuts, cotton

Livestock: Cattle/calves, sheep/lambs, hogs/pigs, chickens

Manufactured products: Food processing, ships, printing, textiles, electronics, chemicals, rubber, furniture, lumber

Mining products: Crushed stone, sand, gravel, coal

Fishing products: Oysters, clams, crabs, eel, fish

Beverage: Milk

Bird: Northern cardinal, once called "Virginia nightingale"

Boat: Chesapeake Bay deadrise

Dance: Square dance

Dog: American foxhound

Fish: Brook trout

Flower: American dogwood

Fossil: Chesapectin jeffersonius, the first identified North American fossil

Insect: Tiger swallowtail butterfly

Motto: Sic Semper Tyrannis, "Thus always to tyrants"

Nicknames: Old Dominion, Mother of Presidents, Mother of States

Shell: Oyster

Song: None

Tree: American dogwood

Wildlife: Bald eagles, beavers, black bears, blue jays, bobcats, cardinals, catfish, clams, crabs, foxes, herons, humming-birds, minks, mussels, oysters, pelicans, peregrine falcons, rabbits, raccoons, river otters, robins, sea turtles, skunks, snow geese, trout, weasels, wild ponies, woodpeckers

TIMELINE

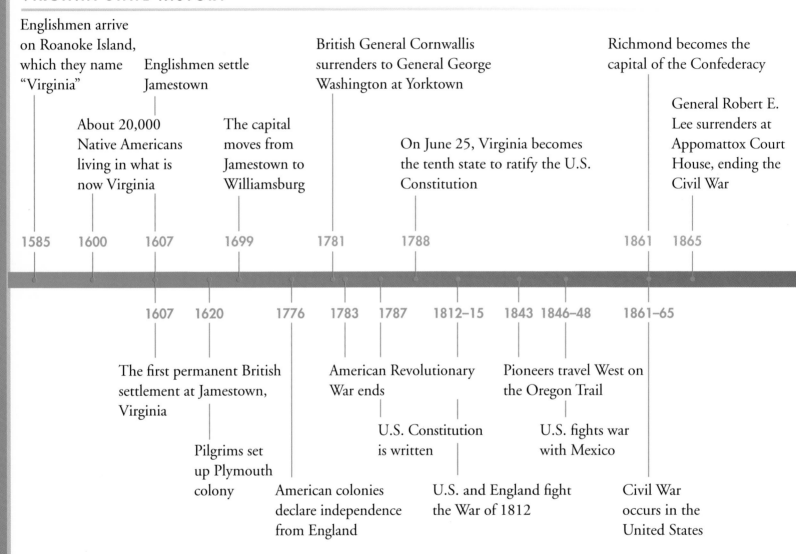

VIRGINIA STATE HISTORY

Englishmen arrive on Roanoke Island, which they name "Virginia"

Englishmen settle Jamestown

About 20,000 Native Americans living in what is now Virginia

The capital moves from Jamestown to Williamsburg

British General Cornwallis surrenders to General George Washington at Yorktown

On June 25, Virginia becomes the tenth state to ratify the U.S. Constitution

Richmond becomes the capital of the Confederacy

General Robert E. Lee surrenders at Appomattox Court House, ending the Civil War

1585   1600   1607   1699   1781   1788   1861   1865

1607   1620   1776   1783   1787   1812–15   1843   1846–48   1861–65

The first permanent British settlement at Jamestown, Virginia

Pilgrims set up Plymouth colony

American colonies declare independence from England

American Revolutionary War ends

U.S. Constitution is written

U.S. and England fight the War of 1812

Pioneers travel West on the Oregon Trail

U.S. fights war with Mexico

Civil War occurs in the United States

UNITED STATES HISTORY

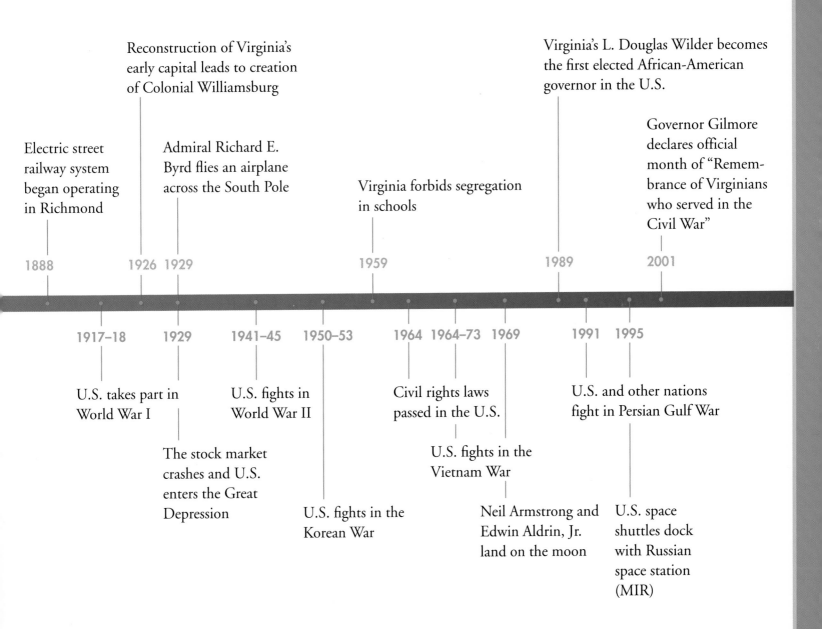

Reconstruction of Virginia's early capital leads to creation of Colonial Williamsburg

Virginia's L. Douglas Wilder becomes the first elected African-American governor in the U.S.

Electric street railway system began operating in Richmond

Admiral Richard E. Byrd flies an airplane across the South Pole

Governor Gilmore declares official month of "Remembrance of Virginians who served in the Civil War"

Virginia forbids segregation in schools

1888   1926 1929   1959   1989   2001

1917–18   1929   1941–45   1950–53   1964 1964–73 1969   1991 1995

U.S. takes part in World War I

U.S. fights in World War II

Civil rights laws passed in the U.S.

U.S. and other nations fight in Persian Gulf War

The stock market crashes and U.S. enters the Great Depression

U.S. fights in the Vietnam War

U.S. fights in the Korean War

Neil Armstrong and Edwin Aldrin, Jr. land on the moon

U.S. space shuttles dock with Russian space station (MIR)

GALLERY OF FAMOUS VIRGINIANS

Arthur Ashe
(1943–1993)
The first African-American man to win U.S. Open title (1968). Born in Richmond.

Sandra Bullock
(1964–)
Popular actress. Born in Arlington.

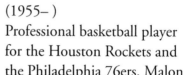

Richard E. Byrd
(1888–1957)
Flew over the North Pole (1926), established a base camp in Antarctica called "Little America," and flew over the South Pole in 1929. The first and only person to fly over both poles. Born in Winchester.

Harry F. Byrd
(1887–1966)
U.S. Senator, governor of Virginia. Brother of Richard E. Byrd. Helped pass the first anti-lynching law, but opposed desegregation. Born in Martinsburg, W. VA.

Katie Couric
(1957–)
Journalist, co-host of NBC's "Today Show." Born in Arlington.

Jerry Falwell
(1933–)
Baptist minister, television preacher. Born in Lynchburg.

Ella Fitzgerald
(1917–1996)
Legendary jazz singer called the "First Lady of Song." Born in Newport News.

Moses Malone
(1955–)
Professional basketball player for the Houston Rockets and the Philadelphia 76ers. Malone retired in 1995 after 21 years. Born in Petersburg.

Cyrus Hall McCormick
(1809–1884)
Invented a mechanical reaper that changed farming by doing the work of a hundred men. McCormick's company still exists as International Harvester. Born in Rockbridge County.

Edgar Allan Poe
(1809–1849)
Developed the detective story genre and wrote poetry, including "The Raven." Raised in Richmond.

Woodrow Wilson
(1856–1924)
Wilson was president of Princeton University, governor of New Jersey, and president of the United States from 1913 to 1921. Born in Staunton.

GLOSSARY

abolitionist: a person who believed in an immediate end to slavery

Bill of Rights: a document that outlines basic rights for citizens

delegates: representatives; people selected to represent others

democratic: of or for the people in general; democracy is government by the people, exercised through representatives

desegregation: the end of racial separation

discrimination: the unfair treatment of people based on their belonging to a certain group

fall line: the border between two of Virginia's natural regions. The land is higher to the west of the fall line, causing many waterfalls and rapids in rivers

indentured servants: people who agree to work for someone for a set period of time to pay a debt

Jim Crow laws: laws that allowed discrimination against African-Americans

lynch: murder committed by a mob, usually by hanging

massive resistance: the practice of closing public schools and opening private ones to resist desegregation

piedmont: an area lying along or near the foot of mountains

plateau: an area of level land that is higher than the surrounding land

poll tax: tax that must be paid before a person can vote

ratify: accept, agree on

segregation: a system of separating people, usually by color or gender

service industries: areas of business that sell services rather than goods

stalactites/stalagmites: rock formations created by mineral deposits and water drips; stalactites hang off cave ceilings; stalagmites grow upwards from cave floors

tourism: the business of providing hotels, restaurants, and entertainment for visitors

unconstitutional: not allowed by a state or federal constitution

FOR MORE INFORMATION

Web sites

The U.S. 50

www.theus50.com

A guide to the fifty states.

Virginia Tourism

www.virginia.org

The official website of Virginia tourism.

State of Virginia Government

www.state.va.us

Official website for the Virginia state government. Lots of information about Virginia, and even a page just for kids.

The Chesapeake Bay Bridge-Tunnel

www.cbbt.com

Information and interesting facts about the world's largest bridge-tunnel complex.

Books

Collier, Christopher, and James Lincoln Collier. *The Paradox of Jamestown, 1585–1700*. New York: Benchmark Books, 1998.

Edwards, Judith. *Nat Turner's Slave Rebellion in American History*. Berkeley Heights, NJ: Enslow Publishers, 2000.

Henry, Marguerite. *Misty of Chincoteague*. New York: Simon and Schuster, 1975. Originally published 1947.

McDaniel, Melissa. *The Powhatan Indians*. Philadelphia: Chelsea House Publishers, 1995.

Addresses

Virginia Historical Society

428 North Boulevard

Richmond, VA 23220

Virginia Chamber of Commerce

9 South Fifth Street

Richmond, VA 23219

Office of the Governor

State Capitol, 3rd Floor

Richmond, VA 23219

INDEX

ABOUT THE AUTHOR

Gina De Angelis is a freelance writer and a mother. She is the author of over a dozen nonfiction books for children and young adults. One of her lifelong hobbies has been exploring historical sites and finding out how people lived in past times. She lives in Williamsburg, Virginia with her daughter. She was an actor and stage manager at the Pennsylvania Renaissance Faire, and volunteered on an archaeological dig at Colonial Williamsburg. Ms. De Angelis holds a master's degree in history from the University of Mississippi.